5 ASSUMPTIONS
ABOUT **GOD**

AND WHY THEY ARE WRONG ≠

Endorsements

I love and appreciate Jeff Bogue so much. What an amazing gift this book will be for generations to come! I recommend it wholeheartedly.

—David Nasser
Author, Pastor, and Senior Vice President of Liberty University

Are you in search of the truth? Are you troubled by the feeling that there has to be more to the Christian faith than escaping hell and being a rule follower? Or are you at times puzzled and overwhelmed by difficulties in life? If you fall into any one of these categories and want a change for the better, then you must read Jeff's book, *Five Assumptions About God and Why They Are Wrong*. From reading this book, I found that Jeff does an excellent job challenging prominent biblical misconceptions, and in response to those misconceptions we, the readers, receive the truth! From the beginning to the end, you will find within the pages of this book guidance, encouragement, and motivation to pursue a life in which you can learn what it truly means, feels, and looks like to follow Jesus and have the abundant life that Christ promises.

—Jerod Cherry
Radio host with ESPN Cleveland and three-time Super Bowl Champion

Am I really going to heaven when I die? And what does God want from me? Talk about an important topic! Jeff is clear, simple, and warm as he uses stories and Scripture to show how simple it is to be a follower. This is a book we will use with those who are not yet Christians and for new believers too. It is well-written and easy to understand with good follow-up questions to consider. I work in the inner city, and this is a tool we will use for teaching people to understand what it means to be a follower. I highly recommend this book.

—ED LEWIS
Executive Director of CE National
and the Urban Hope Training Center, Philadelphia

Jeff's life journey mirrors what many inside and outside the church wrongly assume about what it means to be a Christ follower. Take the journey with Jeff and enjoy a fresh renewal of the love relationship God wants with each of us. I needed the recharge and refocus this little book provides.

—JOSHUA BEERS
Senior Vice President of Student Experience
at Lancaster Bible College

Having been privileged to see this relational view of God lived out in Jeff's life over the past ten years, there is great joy seeing this picture of a loving God in print. Using his authenticity and relational approach, Jeff has painted a wonderful picture of how loving God is and how messed up our assumptions can be. I love the practical steps at the end of each chapter and have benefitted from them greatly as I worked through my own misconceptions about God. Jeff's consistent and persistent nature to go back to the Bible and build his theology from there pulls me in every time.

—Bradley Deetscreek
Lead Pastor of Family Ministry at Grace Church

Through working closely with Jeff, his extraordinary teaching and leadership have greatly influenced my view of God. This brilliant book is an insightful collection of unexpected thoughts, correcting our faulty assumptions about God. I'm excited for every person who picks up this book and discovers the true heart and mind of God.

—Keith Keltner
Young Adult Pastor at Grace Church

Jeff Bogue has done it again! His new book *Five Assumptions About God and Why They Are Wrong* is a clear reflection of the wisdom gained along the journey. In this must-read, you will discover a way to dramatically break through the assumptions holding you back from an authentic relationship with God. I love how this is a book filled with stories I can relate to in my life. As a prominent leader, I am excited to share a resource with someone from my community seeking to understand the heart and mind of God. Jeff, thanks for adding another weapon to my ministry!

—Vinnie Fisher, Esq.
Founder and CEO of Total CEO and Fully Accountable

The power and passion behind our daily walk as followers of Jesus are fundamentally tied to our assumptions about God. If those assumptions are wrong, we find ourselves with little power and minimal passion. With the personal vulnerability that readers have come to appreciate in Pastor Jeff's writings, his book *Five Assumptions About God and Why They Are Wrong* is a timely resource that confronts the God-myths that each of us in some way struggle with. Jesus followers, with the courage to explore this book's scriptural portrayal of the real God, will experience deepened intimacy and passion to live and love as he does.

—Dr. David Ferguson
Great Commandment Network

In his powerful new book, Jeff Bogue transitions the reader's spiritual journey from the head-only assumption of a God who demands compliance to the heart concept of the sacrificial Jesus who loves us. Jesus told us he did not come to condemn us—we're already condemned by our sin—but to rescue us. Pastor Bogue *clearly* shows this. Once the reader comprehends the love of Jesus as Lord and Savior, the motivation to serve him and others becomes their passion. Truly understanding the love of Jesus makes such a difference! Pastor Bogue clearly shows God offering individual salvation and giving life commandments for the best existence possible—following God himself and not bondage to rules. I highly endorse it.

—Dr. Tom Phillips
Vice President, Billy Graham Evangelistic Association and Executive Director, Billy Graham Library

There is so much truth and wisdom packed into this little book! With humor and transparency, Jeff shares practical insights about who God is and how he wants to interact with us. This book is a must read for anyone who has ever been confused about God.

—CLAYTON KING
President of Clayton King Ministries and
Senior Pastor at NewSpring Church

5 ASSUMPTIONS ABOUT GOD

AND WHY THEY ARE WRONG ≠

JEFF BOGUE

BroadStreet
PUBLISHING

BroadStreet Publishing Group, LLC
Racine, Wisconsin, USA
BroadStreetPublishing.com

Five Assumptions About God and Why They Are Wrong
Head & Heart Series: Book 1

Copyright © 2016 Jeff Bogue

ISBN-13: 978-1-4245-5308-2 (softcover)
ISBN-13: 978-1-4245-5309-9 (e-book)

Stock or custom editions of BroadStreet Publishing titles may be purchased in bulk for educational, business, ministry, fundraising, or sales promotional use. For information, please e-mail info@broadstreetpublishing.com.

Cover design by Ede Bittle
Interior by Katherine Lloyd at theDESKonline.com

Printed in the United States of America

16 17 18 19 20 5 4 3 2 1

I want to dedicate this book to Pastor Bob Combs, a man who taught me about God's love, grace, and compassion through his everyday life. Bob, you are an example of a person rooted in truth, motivated by love, and exuding grace. Thank you for your investment in my life. I am honored to build upon the foundation you laid.

Contents

THE PASSION BEHIND THE HEAD AND HEART SERIES

≠

The Head and Heart series is a collection of written works directed toward exploring the mind and heart of Christ.

I believe it's imperative to explain who God is and to make known his love (or heart) for us. It's important to let people know that it's God's desire to work in our lives in a manner that's ultimately for our good. To understand the mind of God, we must first understand his heart. If everyone could come to the basic point of trust that God loves us and wants what's best for us, then God's heart (including all of the hard teachings of Jesus, his directives, and even the confusing parts of the Bible) would become clear and digestible to us.

In order to show the truth of Scripture, we must first demonstrate how the heart behind the directive will give us the things we ultimately want in life. Once that pathway is established, then the mind (or the head) of God becomes clear and logical.

Through the Head and Heart project, we will investigate what God is like, how he loves us, and why he directs us to live in the manner he does. Using narrative teaching, humor, and practical truths that make our lives work better, I will attempt to lead you to a deeper, fully committed interaction with God.

HEAD SPACE
and How to Get the Most
Out of This Book

As you read through *Five Assumptions About God and Why They Are Wrong*, I want to give you space to pause and think through what we're talking about in a deeper and more purposeful way. To that end, my friend David Ferguson and I created sections called "Head Space," which we have placed at the end of each chapter. There you'll find additional quotes from the Bible to look at and think through. You'll also find questions to chew on, suggested prayers, and ideas for conversations you could have around these topics.

Each "Head Space" has three parts: the first part helps you think through your connection with God; the second part focuses on your connection with others; and the third part explores how you might live differently because of what you've learned. You might interact with the Head Space sections alone, with some friends, for a few minutes, or over the course of a few days. However you want to use these guides, I hope they're helpful as you allow your assumptions about God to be challenged on the deepest levels of your head and heart.

Lastly, please check out JeffBogue.org for more thoughts around these topics.

INTRODUCTION

WHO DOESN'T WANT TO GO TO HELL?

W hen I was six years old, I was invited to follow God based on false premises.

A preacher came to my church. As he was preaching—or, you might say, yelling—he asked a very direct question: "Who does not want to go to hell?"

He seemed to be addressing me personally. I thought, *I don't want to go to hell!*

And then the preacher told me what to do in order not to go to hell. "If you don't want to go to hell," he shouted, "come forward right now and receive Jesus as your Savior."

So I did.

In the subsequent months and years, I was taught that following God meant two things: first, you accept Christ as your Savior so you don't go to hell, and second, once you've made that decision, everything else is about keeping the rules that God sets out for you in the Bible. I learned that the Bible is a rule book, an instruction manual. If you follow the rules and instructions properly, you'll stay on the right side of God and you won't go to hell.

If you *don't* follow the rules and instructions properly, then maybe you never even received Christ in the first place. Maybe you are going to go to hell!

"The people who love God will obey his rules. Therefore, the more you obey his rules, the more evident it is that you love God." That's what they told me.

So, I went to church because that was one of the rules. Our family went to church whenever the doors were open because we were very committed to keeping the rules we'd been taught, and we believed that respecting those rules would keep us safe in our relationship with God. Every week at church our pastor would give us a new set of rules, such as:

- You're not allowed to listen to music that isn't written by Christians.
- You're not allowed to drink any alcohol.
- You're not allowed to use tobacco.
- You're not allowed to go dancing.
- You're not allowed to play games that involve playing cards (because playing cards could also be used for poker and gambling).
- You're not allowed to go to the drive-in movies.

As a spiritually sensitive child, I listened to my pastor, and every time he would give me a new rule, I would do my best to follow it.

Yet when I became a teenager, I started to do some of my own math regarding this rule keeping. I realized there were some rules that came straight from the Bible and some rules that were just sort of made up at church; they weren't in the

Bible anywhere. And yet the rules were what we talked about the most when we gathered together.

I often joke that in the little church where I grew up, you couldn't smoke, drink, or chew, or date girls who do. You didn't have to love your fellow man, you just had to be nice to the people who kept the rules. You couldn't smoke because it was bad for your body and it dishonored God—but you were more than welcome to be 150 pounds overweight. You couldn't say certain words—but saying their substitute versions was absolutely fine. You needed to tell everybody about Jesus—except for certain groups of people, because they deserved God's punishment that was coming to them.

How did all that affect me? I learned to fake my relationship with God. Throughout the week, I lived however I wanted to live, did whatever I wanted to do, and was with whomever I wanted to be with.

But when I went to church, I acted like a church person. I knew all the right words to say and how to find all the right answers in the Bible. I knew how to dress. I knew what songs to sing. And I certainly knew how to make it look as if I were keeping the rules.

Nowhere in that process did my heart ever change. Nowhere did I learn to love Jesus. I just kept the rules.

Then something dramatic happened to me when I was a junior in college. I started hanging out with some people who were very bad rule keepers, but very much loved Jesus. I had a friend named Steve, who was a terrible rule keeper. He had long hair, tattoos, pierced ears, and sometimes drank alcohol.

Any one of those might cause the floor to open up and drop you directly into hell. Or so I was taught. Yet Steve did it all.

And he loved Jesus.

Steve was one of the kindest people I'd ever met and one of the most devout followers of Christ I had ever interacted with. He loved to read the Bible, prayed for fun, and was very committed to sexual purity. I never once saw him drunk, heard him say an unkind word, or lose his patience.

The very things Steve was known for were the kinds of things that I felt short-circuited my own interaction with God. I was often impatient and unkind. It was very typical for me to mock or to be cruel to someone.

Yes, I knew the Bible very well and knew how to behave in church. I knew how to switch on my Christianity when it was beneficial for me. But if I was honest, I also knew I really didn't love Christ.

Steve and I were talking one day, and he asked me, "Have you ever accepted Christ as your Savior?"

"Yes," I said. "I was sitting in church when I was a kid and some preacher asked me if I wanted to go to hell or not and I said no. So I accepted Christ as my Savior and now I'm a Christian."

Steve listened, then asked, "What if you're just assuming that's what it means to be a Christ follower? What if working at being a good person is not what God is really looking for?

What if you're following rules instead of following God himself?"

At that moment, I started a journey of spiritual discovery. I began to question if I really knew what it meant to be a follower of Jesus. Was I a Christ follower ... or a committed rule keeper? I was discovering the two were very different.

Before long, I came to a powerful and shocking conclusion: I had been assuming that being a follower of Christ meant wanting to avoid going to hell, and that you needed to work hard to keep the rules if you wanted to keep being his follower. But I learned that ...

Jesus never asked anyone, "Who doesn't want to go to hell?" Instead, the call of Jesus is, "Who will follow me?"

Following Jesus and loving him is very, very different from knowing and keeping rules we think are in the Bible. I started to think about how "loving Jesus" played out in Steve's life. His love for Jesus translated into loving people. His deeply held faith showed up in very practical, even tangible ways.

I started to ask myself some profound questions. I wondered, *If following Jesus means that I love him with all of my heart, soul, mind, and strength, then wouldn't that present itself as me loving my neighbor as myself?* (Matthew 22:37–39).

I began to question whether or not I was a true follower of Jesus.

After all, my heart had never really changed. I never developed genuine, unconditional love for other people. The desire to follow God because I loved him wasn't there.

All that had really happened in my life was that I'd adopted a false assumption that I wasn't going to hell. And I'd decided to keep certain rules at convenient times in order to maintain the false security and reputation that I was a Christian.

So I gave up trying to be a rule keeper.

Once I gave up and surrendered myself to the love of Jesus, I began to love him back. His love for me and mine for him began to define my life. My life began to change radically for the better.

Since then, I have spent most of my adult life trying to understand what it means to fully download the love of Christ into my life, and to embrace the transformation that comes with his love. I continue to discover new ways to love him back. This is a lot different from following a rulebook. I am always learning to hear him better, and he adjusts my assumptions along the way.

Through the pages of this book, I want to explore these ideas with you. I want to tell you some of the ways I heard about and experienced God. I want to talk to you about different, false assumptions I made about my relationship with God.

I wonder if maybe you are making some of the same assumptions I was making. Ask yourself, *what if these assumptions are wrong?*

This will be a journey of discovery. But that one question could change your life as much as it did mine. Could your understanding of the heart and mind of God change as dramatically as mine did?

By the end of this book, could you find yourself overwhelmed by the love of Jesus? Could you become transformed and empowered through your personal relationship with God?

I dare you to find out!

HEAD SPACE

CONNECT WITH GOD

During his last few moments on earth, Jesus had some of his most meaningful conversations with the disciples (the people who followed Jesus' teachings). In one of these conversations, a disciple asked, "We have no idea where you are going, so how can we know the way?" (John 14:5 NLT). The disciple's question clearly revealed how little he knew about Jesus' thoughts and feelings. Jesus responded, "Have I been with you all this time ... and yet you still don't know who I am?" (v. 9).

Be careful how you hear the words above. There was no shame in Jesus' voice. His face wasn't stern or disappointed. Jesus wasn't disgusted or condemning. He was sad. Jesus desperately wanted his disciples to know him, because he loved them! So if you need to, stop, and reread his words:

"Have I been with you all this time ... and yet you still don't know who I am?"

Hear his gentle and compassionate tone?

Now, chew on this idea. Jesus has this same desire for you and for me. He wants us to know him—the real Jesus. He wants us to know his true character, so we can have a close friendship with him.

Think these questions through:

- What assumptions do I sometimes make about God?
- How might I misunderstand God?

Spend the next few minutes talking to God (as you would talk to a close friend). Ask him to bring any wrong assumptions to the surface. Ask him to change your assumptions and allow you to understand Jesus more clearly.

CONNECT WITH OTHERS

Our wrong assumptions about God are, at times, challenged by how others live their lives. Take a couple of minutes and think about how you've seen other people love, forgive, or accept another person. Now consider:

+ Could the story of their lives challenge one of your false assumptions about God? Could their lives show what God is really like?
+ Has there been another person who has impacted your life in such a positive way that you couldn't help but ask the question: Where did he get all of that compassion, kindness, and selflessness? He's the nicest person I know. What if that person was acting on a correct understanding of what God is really like?
+ How might these observations confirm or go against some of your previous assumptions about God's character?

After you've thought about these experiences, you might even want to call or text the people who've made such a positive impact. Thank them for making a difference in your life.

HOW MIGHT I CHANGE?

"Yet the Lord longs to be gracious to you; therefore he will rise up to show you compassion" (Isaiah 30:18). This Bible verse describes one aspect of God. Here are some things you can learn about God from this verse:

- God is *not* out to get you; he loves you even if you don't feel like you deserve it.
- God is *not* focused on how well you are keeping "the rules." Instead, he is focused on having a relationship with you!
- God isn't stuck with you; he looks forward to loving you and showing you compassion.

Imagine this scene playing out in real life: You run into Jesus at a coffee shop and he automatically recognizes that you are having "one of those days." He knows the hard places of your life and everything you are going though. When you sit down, order coffee, and start talking, you notice all of Jesus' responses are kind. At the same time, he's also strong. As you get up to leave, you realize Jesus is a true friend who is really concerned about your life!

If you wanted to live like the "real Jesus"—gracious and compassionate, and moving toward people in need—how might your relationships change? How might you approach people differently?

CHAPTER 1

WRONG ASSUMPTION #1: I NEED TO WORK HARDER TO MAKE GOD HAPPY

$$\neq$$

J ust try harder.

For the longest time, that was how I understood the Christian life. I was convinced that God was watching me, always watching everything I was doing. And I imagined he was not very happy with me most of the time, because I messed up on a regular, almost daily, basis.

I thought God was like my middle school teacher. Let's call her "Miss Jones." Miss Jones was that classic, old, overweight, always-wore-a-dress, and never-got-married schoolteacher. Because she had no real ability to have fun, had no children of her own, and apparently didn't want to be married, she dedicated her life to making my life miserable. At least that's what I believed.

Miss Jones would find every little thing wrong with every little thing I did. She always was watching! She knew when I was talking in class; she knew when I passed a note; she knew when I took a shortcut on my homework; she knew if I stayed out for recess a minute too long. It seemed like Miss Jones knew everything.

I did not like Miss Jones! I thought for sure I had somehow

displeased all the middle school gods, and as a result they had sentenced me to middle school purgatory by making me spend my school year with Miss Jones.

God was like Miss Jones to me. I thought for sure he was out to get me. I could never do enough good for him and I could never hide anything from him. He provoked guilt, shame, and failure on a daily basis. If only I tried harder, maybe I could please him and get on his good side.

What Are Your Assumptions?

I would not be surprised to find that your assumptions about God are a lot like mine were. That's more or less what most of us are taught. I heard things like this: "You'd better knock it off, or you're going to hell." Or, "If you walk into church, the building might collapse on you if you aren't holy enough."

Unfortunately, Christians are often best known for what they do *not* believe in and do *not* agree with.

Christians can come across as very disagreeable people. In our culture today, there are very few people who do not know that Christians stand against gay marriage, for instance. For the most part, Christians have really made a strong point about abortion and euthanasia being wrong. And Christians also have been very boisterous in expressing their political views and in making cultural proclamations about living together before marriage, sexual purity in general, alcohol consumption, and the list goes on.

People could draw the wrong conclusion that there must be a definite set of Christian rules you have to follow, and if you don't align your worldview and behavior with these, then God will be seriously displeased with you.

Christians themselves seem to consistently reinforce that point. Preachers will let you know that many things are very wrong with your life and that one day God's condemnation and judgment will catch up with you, requiring you to pay for your sins in hell.

Now here's where all this gets so confusing: Often, they are actually right! It is absolutely true, for instance, that God teaches us moral standards in the Bible. He is very clear about what our sexual conduct should look like. The Bible tells us what marriage is and is not. Scripture is very clear about many aspects of our behavior.

Both the Old and New Testaments give lists of things that God wants to see play out in our lives. For example:

Get rid of all bitterness, rage and anger, brawling and slander, along with every form of malice. Be kind and compassionate to one another, forgiving each other, just as in Christ God forgave you. Follow God's example, therefore, as dearly loved children and walk in the way of love, just as Christ loved us and gave himself up for us as a fragrant offering and sacrifice to God.

But among you there must not be even a hint of sexual immorality, or of any kind of impurity, or of greed, because these are improper for God's holy people. Nor should there be obscenity, foolish talk or coarse joking, which are out of place, but rather thanksgiving. For of this you can be sure: No immoral, impure or greedy person—such a person is an idolater—has any inheritance in the kingdom of Christ and of God. Let no one deceive you with empty words, for because of such things God's wrath comes on those who are disobedient. (Ephesians 4:31–32; 5:1–6)

Too often when we hear Scriptures like that, we really hone in on the fact that we are supposed to get rid of certain things in our lives—bitterness, rage, anger, slander, sexual immorality, and other things the Bible clearly says are wrong.

When we read such passages, those lists of sins become the only thing we remember.

And when they get amplified by Christian teaching and preaching, it is easy to understand why we would get the idea that God is watching, always watching. You better watch out, buddy—God is watching you and he is going to punish you for every slipup.

That was the message I heard growing up. Every time I went to church and even when I went to school, I heard that God was watching me every minute. And when I slipped up and fell short, or simply disobeyed, I was under the impression that my sins kept piling up. My understanding was that if I sinned too much—if I wound up with too many demerits—then God would withdraw his love from me and I would be forever sentenced to hell and separated from God.

In other words, I believed that there are rules to be followed, and God is not happy when people break them; therefore, I had better spend my life trying harder to make God happy.

Fundamentally Flawed

The Bible teaches us that Jesus, the only Son of God, is perfect. Jesus never sinned. Imagine: he never lied, never acted selfishly, never violated the directives of the Bible or the instruction of his Father, God. He achieved perfection during his days on earth.

Knowing this to be true of God, and knowing I was not even close to perfect, I realized I had a lot of ground to cover from where I was, to where God stood. At different points in my young life, I would try hard to straighten myself up. I would grab the list of rules and would try my very best to rid myself of the behaviors that displeased God.

Now here is the fundamental flaw in that idea: I can't do it! And neither can you. I can't live a perfect life; I cannot live without sinning. It's impossible! If I follow that approach to its logical conclusion, then I'm toast.

It is completely impossible for me to live a perfect life, even if I try harder every day. I will always fail an inspection by a perfect God.

If God is looking for faults and failures in my life and he is trying to uncover wrongdoing in my life, of course he's going to find sin in abundance. I am often selfish. I am greedy. I have sexually impure thoughts … and the list goes on. It is not hard at all to look at my life and know I'm a sinner.

Far from perfect.

As you learn about the core teachings of the Bible, you discover something that Christian teachers refer to as "the gospel." The word *gospel* simply means "good news," but the full meaning of the gospel is a matter of spiritual life and death to you and me. The gospel of Jesus is the good news that he loved us so deeply he was willing to voluntarily rescue us from our sin.

This is where the preachers I heard growing up were exactly right. I, in fact, am a sinner who cannot be good enough to go to heaven. The Bible teaches that "the wages of sin is death" (Romans 6:23). This death is what it means to be sent to hell. My sin is my rebellion against God and will lead me away from him, ultimately to an eternal separation defined by punishment, judgment, and suffering. This fact is indisputable, but what do we do about this problem? Try harder?

The question that arises is this: If, by trying hard enough, I *could* live a perfect life and rid myself of all sin, then why would I need God's forgiveness? If, by my own efforts, I could make all the sin in my life go away, if I could follow the rules perfectly, if I could earn my own way to heaven by doing enough good deeds, then why did Jesus have to intervene on my behalf and die for me?

I wrestled with that question for a long time. It didn't make any sense. If I was supposed to make a relationship with God happen by myself, why did Jesus have to make it happen for me?

For the Love of God

I find it fascinating that the Bible talks about Jesus being our atoning sacrifice, which means that Jesus died in our place.

Jesus paid a debt he did not owe for a debt I cannot pay.

The fancy church term for that is *substitutionary atonement.* Jesus is our substitute, "the Lamb of God, who takes away the sin of the world" (John 1:29). He died for a sin-filled me so I don't have to atone for my own sins.

This is the whole point of Jesus living a perfect earthly life, dying an innocent death, and then rising from the dead. I am a sinner and I cannot live a perfect life, no matter how hard I try. It's a simple but profound fact: my sins separate me from God and yet God, "not wanting anyone to perish, but everyone to come to repentance" (2 Peter 3:9) and wanting to close the impossible gap between himself and us, intervened. He sent his Son, Jesus. All of this was because of his unconditional love for us. He initiated what we could not initiate on our own—a rescue effort! In his sinless life, innocent death, and resurrection, Jesus was demonstrating his power over sin and his exceedingly great love for us!

A famous Bible verse from the book of John talks about this. Maybe you've heard or seen John 3:16. It goes like this: "For God so loved the world that he gave his one and only Son, that whoever believes in him shall not perish but have eternal life." That concise verse sums up exactly what had to happen: I am a sinner who cannot live a perfect life. So God sent his Son, Jesus, to live a perfect life then give himself as a sacrifice for me. If I accept Jesus' sacrifice, my sins will be forgiven and I will be rescued.

I love that verse. But, my favorite verse is actually the next one, John 3:17. It goes like this: "For God did not send his Son into the world to condemn the world, but to save the world through him." To me, that is one of the most powerful things the Bible has to say!

What it means is this: God did not send Jesus to run an inspection on my life. Jesus is not lurking around waiting for me to fail. He is not scrutinizing my life—watching, always watching.

Jesus came into the world to save me precisely because I have already failed my inspection!

Jesus did not come into the world to condemn the world; we have already condemned ourselves by not living a perfect life. Our sin condemns us; we don't measure up to the standards of our holy God, who has such a pure love that he doesn't accept a hint of evil. We've all sinned, every single one of us, sometimes by accident but usually on purpose.

Let's be honest.

God knows full well that you and I are sinners. That's the point! He knows we will fall short of his glorious standard. He knows that none of us can live a perfect life. He knows that you and I will continue to sin, both intentionally and unintentionally. And that's why he sent his Son to rescue you and me—to save the world.

This is the good news—the gospel!

What if following God is *not* about trying harder? What if following God is not about getting our acts together? What if following God is not about us working harder and harder, trying to make God happy with us? What if all you and I have to do is *receive* his love and the forgiveness that he knows full well we need?

"For God So Loved the World ..."

When the realization hit me that God was not out to get me, but rather he was out to *love* me, it was life changing. I remember hearing, *You have failed inspection—yet God loves you anyway*, in the context of "while we were still sinners, Christ died for us" (Romans 5:8). That truth caused me to interact with God in a completely different way.

I exist so God can *love* me? Seriously, that's *it*? It must be the case, because of the wording of John 3:16—"For God so loved the world...."

Once I realized that God loves me in spite of my sin, I quit hiding my sin from God.

I started to openly confess my sin to God and reach out to him for help to overcome my sin, weaknesses, and struggles instead of pretending I didn't have any. Now remember, I was not raised to think this way at all, so this was a very difficult transition. I had no model to follow.

I told you earlier that I grew up going to a church that emphasized following the rules. What that meant, in practical terms, was that if you had a problem, the *last* people you would ever tell would be the people you went to church with, because they would judge you and label you a sinner condemned by God. End of story.

When I got ahold of the truth that God was out to love me, and that he was not only willing to forgive me for my sins but also to *help me overcome my failures*, something dramatic happened in my relationships with other Christ followers. I started to confess my sin to them, asking them to pray for me and to remind me of God's truth *and* God's love.

I no longer had to live the two-faced life of hiding my sin and pretending it didn't exist.

Now I could live an authentic life where I could strip away my plastic facade that said, *I'm okay* all the time, and I could "live naked" and be the person I really am, knowing I'm loved by God! (I talk more about this in my book *Living Naked: How an Ordinary Person Can Live an Extraordinary Life*.)

Wrong Assumptions Are Wrong

Remember Miss Jones? I've never been so wrong about a person as I was about Miss Jones. The year I was in her class, my dad had a stroke. This blew up my family's whole world. I was a scared twelve-year-old kid who was suddenly missing a lot of school and going home every day to a family that had been shaken to its very core because our rock, my dad, had become weakened through sickness. Do you know who cared about me, helped me, and prayed with me the most? You guessed it—Miss Jones.

In her old-fashioned way with her old-fashioned methods and old-fashioned faith, she put her arm around a scared twelve-year-old boy. She stayed late at her desk to help me catch up with my schoolwork. I started going to class early just because I knew she would ask me, "How are you doing, Jeff?" Oftentimes I would be the last one to go out to recess because I knew she would take a minute to put her arm around me and pray for me.

I grew to love and appreciate her very deeply. Without her, I'm not really sure I would have made it through that school year. Miss Jones wasn't out to get me after all—she was there because she loved me. Did she hold me to a standard? Of course. Did she often address my inappropriate behavior? Certainly. Did she care? Was she willing to help? Was she a person I learned to go to instead of hide from? Oh, yes.

Did she do all of that because she loved me?

Absolutely!

God is not out to get you either! He loves you. He came for you, and wants to build a friendship with you, walking and talking in the ordinary moments of your everyday life.

CONNECT WITH GOD

Life brings situations, circumstances, and even people who are not perfect. The good news is God loves us even while we're imperfect. Scripture reminds us that "God demonstrates his own love toward us, in that while we were yet sinners, Christ died for us" (Romans 5:8 NASB).

Jesus already knows the whole story. He can see every time, choice, situation, and relationship where you've been less than perfect. He knows every regret. And yet, even while Jesus knew every detail of the sin and imperfection in your life, he chose to die for you. He loves you, despite your behavior; he loves you, flaws and all! That's what it means to love unconditionally.

Take a few moments and think through some of your more imperfect moments. What are your weaknesses? When have you messed up or made choices that you regret? How does that make you feel—to know that, despite your imperfections, God says you are worth his love? How do you feel knowing that Jesus proved you are worth dying for? How might God want to demonstrate this same unconditional love to others through you?

Pray this prayer:

When I reflect on the fact that you love me, God, and I'm valuable enough that you'd let Jesus die for me, I feel …

CONNECT WITH OTHERS

Jesus told his disciples, "Everyone who is fully trained will be like their teacher" (Luke 6:40). As a Jesus follower, we strive to become like our Teacher, Jesus. The Bible teaches us that Jesus is:

- The only true Teacher. (Matthew 23:10)
- The one who is love. (1 John 4:8)
- The God of all comfort. (2 Corinthians 1:3–4)
- The one who is "gentle and humble in heart." (Matthew 11:29)
- The one who is moved with compassion because of the needs of people. (Luke 15:20)
- The one who encourages you through Scripture. (Romans 15:4)
- The one who bears your burdens daily and supports you in life's struggles. (Galatians 6:2)

Jesus asks you to express his love to hurting people. He invites you to be changed by his love, so you can reflect it to the people around you.

Is God pushing you to become more _____ (comforting, gentle, compassionate, encouraging, supportive, or attentive) to those in your life?

Get rid of any distractions for a minute and have this honest conversation with God:

In what ways do you want me to change? Change me, because I want to become more like you so that …

HOW MIGHT I CHANGE?

It's mind-blowing to realize it was the intensity of God's love for us that drove him to give us Jesus to pay for our sin! In John 3:16, he said, "For God so loved the world that he gave his one and only Son, that whoever believes in him shall not perish but have eternal life." Jesus' words were incredible and his miracles were amazing, but the things he said and did were meant to call attention to how he loved. Just look at a few examples of Jesus' love:

- He loved people with leprosy by healing their bodies and bringing dignity to their lives. Jesus even touched people who were contagious with deadly diseases, in order to heal them. (Luke 5:12, 13; 17:11–19)
- He loved a Samaritan woman when he broke all cultural rules by asking her for a drink of water. In the middle of her embarrassment and rejection, he forgave her and told her how to get into heaven. (John 4:4–26)
- He loved a woman caught in adultery by kneeling down beside her, sympathizing with her, and protecting her life. He pushed back against her accusers and offered forgiveness to her as he lovingly said, "Woman, where are they? Has no one condemned you? Neither do I condemn you. Go now and leave your life of sin." (John 8:10, 11)

Jesus' love was radical. His unconditional love even upset religious people because they couldn't believe he would forgive such big offenses and display such compassion towards sinful people.

Stop and think about how Jesus' love shows up in your life. When did his love first intrigue you? How do you see God's love showing up every day? What are some ways you could express this radical love to the people around you?

CHAPTER 2

WRONG ASSUMPTION #2: ALL GOD WANTS ME TO DO IS GO TO CHURCH

≠

≠

When I was growing up, my family went to church three or four times a week. My parents were very loving and devoted to each other, their children, and God. To them, that meant taking us to the church building as often as possible.

We attended service on Sunday mornings and went back again for another one Sunday night. On Wednesday evenings, our family went to church for the midweek Bible study and prayer time. And almost every week, some special meeting or special event drew us back to the church for a fourth time. Despite whatever else was going on in our lives, we did not miss church.

Church was like a second home to me. In some ways, that was refreshing, but in other ways, it was draining.

Even When It's Below Freezing

Once a year, without fail, our family got up extra early so we could celebrate Easter Sunday—not in the church building, but outside, on the lawn. It was called the sunrise service, and yes, it happened at dawn. I'm talking about Easter Sunday in

Ohio, where in late March or early April it's not uncommon for the outside temperature to only be in the teens.

Rows of metal folding chairs would have been set up on the grass under the bare trees. The congregation would shuffle in, bundled in winter coats on top of their Easter finery. We would sit outside and sing songs and read Scripture in the freezing cold until the sun came up. Somehow—I was never quite sure how—this was supposed to help us celebrate Jesus rising from the dead.

To be honest, it never really worked for me. I just shivered and hunkered down into the collar of my coat. My teeth chattered as the cold metal of the chair numbed my bottom. It was like sitting on a block of ice. By the time the sun came up, I was in the beginning stages of hypothermia, no longer able to stand to my feet.

The Easter sunrise service was organized with the best of intentions by people who loved Jesus and wanted to help other people love Jesus. But it had almost the opposite effect on me. When I grew up and started working as a pastor, I committed to never put my congregation through that. Never again would I lead or attend a sunrise service, so help me God!

Do or Die

My family's faithful attendance at the sunrise service was only one manifestation of a mind-set based on the wrong assumption that a Christian must go to church all the time in order to please God. Traditions differ from church to church, but any of them can lull people into thinking that the sum total of the Christian life is physical participation in services and events.

Some people go to church every single day for Mass or Communion. Some people only show up on Christmas and Easter or just once a year for confession. Others play all their sports, experience their entire social lives, and even attend school in a church building.

There's nothing wrong with any of those things, as long as they're not being done to garner God's favor.

But too often the unspoken assumption goes something like this: the more I am ingrained into the life of the church and the more religious activities I participate in, the more pleasing I am to God.

What is the end result of this type of thinking? For me, the result was becoming a very religious person who participated in all kinds of religious activities. But you know what? You can be a very religious person and not love Jesus at all. That's definitely the way it worked for me.

As I grew up, I went to church every week and here was my thinking:

Throughout the week I will run up a balance on my spiritual credit card, and then, by going to church, I will pay that balance off.

That was really what my relationship with God was like. It wasn't about me loving God, being committed to him, or even wanting to know him. It was all about how much I could get away with and then how quickly I could make everything good again by running back to church.

Have you done this?

Many of us view God this way. For some people, it's because of being raised, as I was, in a religious home. For others, it's just the way they think religion works. By definition, people who are into religion are people who go to church, right? In our culture, even going to church only a couple times a year qualifies you as a religious person.

God with Us

Is "being religious" the same as knowing God? It is really fascinating when you start digging into the Bible to find out what God says about how people should follow him. Before long,

you discover that going to church all the time is actually *not* what God has in mind.

If that's all he wanted from us, I don't think the Father would have given his Son, Jesus, to die on the cross. In the Bible, Jesus is also called Immanuel, which means "God with us" (Matthew 1:23).

A God who is *with us* is very different from a God who is apart from us and wants people to pay homage to him. God actually wants to spend time with us. He wants to have a friendship and talk with us every day. He wants to live life with us in the midst of the weeds of our normal everyday comings and goings. That does not sound like a distant, disapproving God who needs to be placated by weekly visits to church. I am a pastor, so as you can guess, I am pro church attendance.

Please don't misunderstand what I'm driving at here. Going to church is a huge part of our relationship with God and his people. Most people go to church for the right reasons; they want to connect more deeply in their relationship with Christ and serve the people of the church and their community. But God never intended the gathering of the church to be a dry, repetitious, laborious obligation. The gathering of the church should be a life-giving activity that enhances our relationship with God and other Christ followers. God never intended church attendance to be a spiritual credit card payment.

Jesus wants us to be his friends. How do I know this? From his own words: "I no longer call you servants, because a servant does not know his master's business. Instead, I have called you friends, for everything that I learned from my Father I have made known to you" (John 15:15). This is the truth.

Far from demanding that his followers perform certain rituals at certain times, Jesus wants to have a relationship. He wants to do things for us and help us.

Here's a more complete picture of Jesus:

Who, being in very nature God,
    did not consider equality with God something to
be used to his own advantage;
    rather, he made himself nothing
    by taking the very nature of a servant,
    being made in human likeness.

And being found in appearance as a man,
    he humbled himself
    by becoming obedient to death—
        even death on a cross! (Philippians 2:6–8)

What makes us think that a Savior like this wants the people he's rescued to spend so much of their time sitting in a church pew (or on a metal folding chair) to endure an obligation meant to appease him? He is a *relational* God. The church of a relational God should be a gathering of like-minded people who love God and want to spend time with Him. This type of church has passion for hurting people and will sacrifice deeply to help them realize their personal need for forgiveness and Christ's eagerness to forgive. That's why going to church should be an exciting event, not a time of dread, punishment, or attempting a self-saving performance that leads nowhere.

God wants to know you, and he wants you to know him. He wants to "do life" with you. From the very beginning of the Bible, we see that God created Adam and Eve so he could be with them daily. The first chapter of the first book of the Bible, Genesis, paints a picture of God strolling in the garden in the cool of the evening. A God who loved being with the man and woman he created, talking, laughing, and sharing the magnificent variety of plants and animals he created.

Then sin came into the human experience, and sin is what separated us from God. The rest of the Bible is one big, long story of God reaching out to the human beings he created, giving them one opportunity after another to get free from their sin so their strong relationship with God could be restored.

By Appointment Only?

My beautiful wife, Heidi, is the joy and love of my life. I love spending time with her because she is one of the happiest, most adventurous, and fun-to-be-with people you could ever hope to meet. I love talking with her. I love going places with her. I love the life that we live together.

I'd never be able to have a good or close relationship with Heidi if our relationship was defined by a one-hour weekly appointment.

Can you imagine a marriage or even a friendship that was completely based on a weekly one-hour-long meeting on, say, Sunday morning?

And after reaching the one-hour mark, the two parties would really not think about each other or interact in any way for the rest of the week. But the next Sunday, they would come back and meet again for exactly one hour. That whole idea is ridiculous.

And yet that is often the way we conduct our relationship with God.

Why would God step out of heaven and come to earth, put skin on, and live in the human experience so we could relate to him? Why did he choose to actually die for us, rise from the dead, and make a way for us to get to know his heart and mind through the Bible and make it possible for us to talk to him directly through prayer—only to limit his relationship with us to a one-hour weekly appointment?

Why should God go to all that trouble to make a relationship possible, only to restrict it to a few rigidly scheduled times and places? How could such a relationship possibly grow and flourish?

He didn't and it can't.

Too many of us have made wrong assumptions about God. While it's absolutely true that followers of Jesus should regularly (even weekly) meet together, maybe it's not true that God is expecting people to show up once a week to pay homage to him. Maybe that's not what he's looking for. In fact, I'm sure that's not what he's looking for at all.

God is looking for people who want to go through life with him, talk with him, and love him every moment of every day. Instead of going to church to gain points with God, he invites his followers to gather together once or twice a week so they can learn to love and serve each other. Through serving each other, they recognize and reflect how Jesus, with his servant's heart, gave his life for them.

God with Us!

It took a while for all of that to dawn on me, but when it did, it was absolutely life changing.

God wants to spend time with me! He wants to be my friend!

My old way of treating him as some big religious force out in the cosmos had to change.

God wants to interact with me day in and day out. He loves me more than any earthly friend—even more than my wife does. The least I can do is stop treating him like a heavenly credit card.

Now I no longer go to church out of guilt or obligation. That's gone. Now I hang out all day with my friend named Jesus. I talk with him through prayer. In the Bible we are encouraged to "pray without ceasing" (1 Thessalonians 5:17 NASB). I hear from him as often as I want to by reading the Bible, through which he most clearly expresses his heart and mind. And I love to gather together once or twice a week with other Christ followers to express my love for them, be involved in their lives, and to worship and pray to the God we all serve.

I would never have said this when I was fourteen, fifteen, or even twenty years old, but now, after gaining this realization about God's love, I can honestly say I look forward to going to church. When I'm in a church service, I no longer watch the clock. I no longer dread walking through the door, wondering how long it's going to last. I no longer get up halfway through the music to go to the bathroom. I no longer play tic-tac-toe on the back of my bulletin.

Now, because I go to church with my close friend Jesus, I enjoy my time there. I may get blown away by a new insight from the Bible and I know I'll get many reminders about God's love. I get energized by connecting with God's people. What great fun it is to follow Jesus together!

HEAD SPACE

CONNECT WITH GOD

What does friendship look like? Jesus said, "I no longer call you servants, because a servant does not know his master's business. Instead, I have called you friends, for everything that I learned from my Father I have made known to you" (John 15:15). Jesus thinks of his followers as his friends.

How does real friendship play out?

- *Friends know each other deeply*. Jesus knows you, and you reciprocate the friendship by making it a priority to know him. (Jeremiah 1:5; Philippians 3:8)
- *Friends initiate care for one another*. Jesus meets needs. (Matthew 15:29–31; Philippians 4:19)
- *Friends are committed to each other*. Jesus is committed to you. (Psalm 37:25; 85:8; 139:3)
- *Friends trust each other with their deepest thoughts and feelings*. Jesus shares his joys, hurts, and hopes. (John 15:11, 18; 17:5)

Jesus shared everything with his friends because he loved them. He chose to love you as well and wants to share his life with you. How might your connection to God deepen if you thought of him more as a friend?

CONNECT WITH OTHERS

Jesus wants us to interact with him as a friend. As our friendship with God deepens, it will spill over into our friendships with the people around us. This is a big part of how we express God's love to the people in our daily paths of life.

The Bible says: "No one has ever seen God; but if we love each other, God lives in us and his love is complete in us" (1 John 4:12). God's love is played out in our relationships with others. Not only should we love others, but we also need to allow others to love us. This idea goes both directions.

It's through the love of other people in our lives that we are able to understand what it's like to be loved by God.

Take a look at these Bible verses:

- Accept one another, then, just as Christ accepted you, in order to bring praise to God. (Romans 15:7)
- Praise be to the God and Father of our Lord Jesus Christ, the Father of compassion and the God of all comfort. (2 Corinthians 1:3)

Lastly, chew on this: How does God use people to express his love to others? Who, in the pattern of your life, needs to experience encouragement, comfort, acceptance, or support through you?

HOW MIGHT I CHANGE?

Some people struggle to understand why God gave us the Bible. Even the religious leaders in Jesus' day struggled to understand its purpose. They memorized parts of Scripture, but the words never went from their heads to their hearts. They did things that looked righteous, but God's words and his love never changed their lives. They sought God, but never really understood his heart or mind.

The same thing happens today. Many people know parts of the Bible, but how many of them are really trying to follow it? If all supposedly religious people implemented the Bible's teachings in their lives, the world would look a lot different.

How do you get the Bible out of your head and into your heart? This is one of the main jobs of the Holy Spirit. When Jesus' time on earth was ending, he told his disciples he wouldn't be with them for a while, but he would send his Holy Spirit in his place (John 14:26). The Spirit was given to Jesus' followers to help guide them in life since Jesus wouldn't be around to do that in person.

When we read the Bible, it's the Holy Spirit who helps us move the truth of the Bible from our heads to our hearts. Here's an exercise I suggest to help you allow this process to happen:

- Read John 9 three times. (If you don't have a Bible, search online for John chapter 9 in the NIV version.)
- The first time through, read it just to get the information and then answer the question: *What does the Bible even say in John 9?*
- Read it again. This time through answer the following questions:

  What is God like?
  - Is he sad or happy?
  - What is he upset about?
  - What is he happy about?
  - What type of friend is he?
  - Who is he talking to?

- Is he tired?
- Is he frustrated?

- Read it a final time and answer the question: *If Jesus is like that, and I want to be like Jesus, how should my heart and mind change?*

CHAPTER 3

WRONG ASSUMPTION #3: GOD WILL NEVER BE HAPPY WITH ME

≠

Have you ever had to deal with a hard-to-satisfy organization or person? Something is always wrong. Somehow, you just cannot make them happy.

Maybe you've gone to register for school and you have filled out all the forms online so you could send it in to the registrar, only to be told you're missing one. So you find the missing form and resend it. And then you're told you're missing one more, so you fill it out and send it, only to be told you're missing yet another one. By the time you finally get through that long, frustrating process you may not even want to go to that school anymore.

I'm sure you know what I'm talking about, because every one of us has been stuck with a system or a person we just cannot seem to make happy. Sometimes the situation is merely frustrating, but other times it is downright infuriating. It's as if someone shows you a target and you aim for it—only to have them move the target to another location.

Someone says, "Here is the bar; jump over this bar," and while you're jumping as high and as hard as you possibly can, they raise the bar while you're in midair.

It's not fair. It feels dishonest. After that kind of exasperation, you can start to feel too defeated to try anymore and may just give up.

Always More Demands

That was what my relationship with God was like. By my early twenties, I felt defeated in my efforts to keep him happy.

Here is how it developed: I grew up with other people's opinions about God affecting my view of God, which is pretty normal. Most of us form our view of God through some type of religious experience as interpreted by the people around us. What your parents, grandparents, pastor, or priest told you about God is what you have come to believe. Or if those who taught you about God had a negative effect on your life, maybe you formed your view of God by disbelieving them—concluding they're not good people, so their information must be bad also. Either way, other people affect our view of God more than we know.

There is nothing really wrong with learning about God that way—except when what you're being taught about God is incorrect, which is what happened to me. As I grew up attending church services and going to a religious school,

I learned a lot of information about God, and most of that information was correct. Factually correct. Yet very little of that information had been filtered through the mind and heart of God.

The information was simply presented to me as facts: This is what God is like. This is what God has to say.

The facts may have been correct, but the application was tainted. The people in my life interpreted those facts about God and what he tells us in the Bible through their own lens. In fact, for the most part, they applied the statements of the Bible as accusations. They led me to believe the reason people are supposed to follow the Bible is to keep God happy, and that people (like me) who failed to measure up to those standards would stand guilty as charged.

I would hear them say, for instance, "The Bible does not allow sexual immorality. You are living a sexually immoral life. You are offending God," or, "The Bible says you shouldn't get drunk on wine. You drink wine. You should stop," or "The Bible says that no unwholesome talk should come out of your mouth. You use bad words. That displeases the Lord."

As I was growing up, I was a fairly spiritually sensitive kid. I actually cared about what the Bible said and wanted to please God and the people in my life. So when they told me that something was wrong with me and I needed to fix it, I generally paid attention and then tried to correct it.

All the way through my childhood and early teenage years, I worked very, very hard to keep everyone, including God, happy with me.

Someone told me I was not supposed to listen to rock-and-roll music, so I quit listening to rock-and-roll music. Someone told me I was not supposed to say any swear words, so I quit saying swear words. Someone told me I was supposed to be nice to old ladies, so I was nice to old ladies. Someone told me I was supposed to be respectful to adults, so I was respectful to adults. And the list went on and on and on (you get the picture).

As I got older, I began to notice a pattern, and by the time I got to college, I was sure of it:

> **Every time I began to fix one thing in my life that the Bible said was wrong, I would go to church and hear about three *new* things that were wrong with me and my life.**

The longer I endured this pattern, the more I understood the impossible situation it put me in. God would never be happy with me. My spiritual life had become a hopeless cycle of trying, having the bar raised, trying harder, then having the bar raised even higher. This went on and on until I got more than frustrated; I felt discouraged, disillusioned, and defeated about living the Christian life to the point that I gave up.

What's the point? I wondered. *I'm trying to please God, and every time I do something to please him, he raises the bar and makes it impossible for me to succeed.*

I quit caring what God thought, what the Bible said, and whether I was listening to other followers of Christ or not. I threw my hands up and thought to myself, *I am serving a dysfunctional spiritual Father who cannot be pleased. Therefore, I might as well go do my own thing. Why even try anymore?* I was working as hard as possible trying to make God happy, but he still viewed me as a sinner. Why bother making all of this effort to try to be a good person when I would always be considered a bad person anyway?

So I walked away from trying so hard to please God. I stopped allowing God's mind and heart to affect my life. While I still attended church services and tried to be polite in religious settings, in the depths of my heart I didn't care anymore about trying to please God with my behavior. I didn't even want to think about getting my act together, because I knew as soon as I turned my attention back to such things I would only learn about more things I was doing wrong. "Being good" was a burden I was not willing to lug around anymore.

Heavy or Light?

One day, I discovered that Jesus said something very interesting about what it means to follow him. He said:

"Come to me, all you who are weary and burdened, and I will give you rest. Take my yoke upon you and learn from me, for I am gentle and humble in heart, and you will find rest for your souls. For my yoke is easy and my burden is light" (Matthew 11:28–30).

I remember reading those words—and not believing them. To me, following Jesus had always meant *burdens*. Following Jesus meant carrying the burden of being a good person, the burden to remember everything the Bible says, the burden of going to church every week, and the burden of getting my act together.

> **Following Jesus was burdensome. I'd tried it, and it hadn't worked. It was too much and made me weary. I was done.**

When we look again at the passage from Matthew, it's easy to wonder if it was even translated correctly. The words seem weirdly contradictory: "My yoke is easy and my burden is light." How can a yoke be easy to have around your neck? How can a burden be light?

To see a photograph of an actual yoke, you can search online for images of oxen yoke. Asian rice farmers still use a pair of oxen teamed with a yoke for plowing. The yoke is a big wooden contraption that gets fastened around the neck of two animals. It causes them to walk in unison with each other and share the burden of pulling a load that would be too heavy for one ox to pull alone. A yoke is fairly heavy, confining, and uncomfortable, and is certainly not something I would want around my neck.

So why does Jesus refer to his yoke as "easy" and "light"?

To help our understanding, we need to time travel back to Jesus' time. In the first century, the word *yoke* referred to the kind used with pairs of oxen, but it was also used to talk about students, who were often referred to as disciples. In Bible times, disciples followed their masters (or rabbis) everywhere in order to learn everything the master could teach him. They'd eventually learn to think like, talk like, act like, and view the world like their master. As the master philosophized about the Scriptures, for example, he would teach his disciples how to apply the words of Scripture to their lives. He'd also model what he was teaching them, so they could visualize how to follow God.

After a disciple had been completely engaged with his master's teaching and lifestyle for a long time, his master's influence would show. Then people who met that disciple would say, "You have taken the yoke of your master." In other words, "Now you act like, talk like, think like, and view the world just as your master does. The two of you are pretty much indistinguishable from each other."

So when Jesus says his yoke (his teaching) is easy and his burden is light, part of what he's saying is becoming like him is a benefit to you.

As you act like, think like, and live like Jesus, your life will become truly meaningful, satisfying, and even happy.

This is deeply illustrated in Matthew 5:3–12, where Jesus gives us the Beatitudes, a list of things that will make us happy:

> "Blessed are the poor in spirit,
>   for theirs is the kingdom of heaven.
> Blessed are those who mourn,
>   for they will be comforted.
> Blessed are the meek,
>   for they will inherit the earth.

Blessed are those who hunger and thirst for righteousness,
for they will be filled.
Blessed are the merciful,
for they will be shown mercy.
Blessed are the pure in heart,
for they will see God.
Blessed are the peacemakers,
for they will be called children of God.
Blessed are those who are persecuted because of
righteousness,
for theirs is the kingdom of heaven.
Blessed are you when people insult you, persecute
you and falsely say all kinds of evil against you
because of me. Rejoice and be glad, because great
is your reward in heaven, for in the same way they
persecuted the prophets who were before you."

Knowing the word *blessed* means "happy," I find it fascinating to read through this teaching and see that what Jesus
says will make us happy is almost the exact opposite of what
we tend to think will make us happy.

**If we read through the passage in Matthew
again with this new understanding we can
hear Jesus say, "Take up my teachings and
learn from me, for I am gentle and humble
in heart. You will become like me if you
follow me."**

However, this was not the message I grew up with, nor the Jesus I had been following. Jesus' self-description in Matthew 11 stood in direct contrast to my understanding about God. I understood God to be a taskmaster who was never satisfied. But as I began to read the Bible with new eyes, I started to catch a glimpse of the real heart and mind of God.

You Don't Have to Get Your Act Together

I was amazed. I had always thought Jesus said, "If you are heavily burdened, you need to shoulder even more burdens." But the whole time, he was saying, "To be my follower, you *don't* have to get your act together, or be in charge of purifying your own life. You *don't* have to start doing all the right things to qualify for a place as one of my disciples. And you *don't* have to become a good person."

In fact, *you can't!* That's the whole point. As I said in chapter 1, you cannot be a perfect person.

You can't follow the Scriptures perfectly. It's impossible to do everything perfectly on your own.

None of us can. That's why we need Jesus! He knows that none of us can get our act together no matter how hard we might try. So he did it for us, and then he shared his life with us. Jesus didn't want anyone to perish (2 Peter 3:9), so he laid down his life so you and I wouldn't need to pay the punishment for our sins.

Jesus' yoke is light because he does all the hard work for us! The good news is that I don't have to work hard at the impossible task of becoming like God. All I have to do is believe Jesus is who he says he is and receive the forgiveness he offers. God will help me change! God will renew my mind. Christ will make me a "new creation" as I follow him (2 Corinthians 5:17).

The Bible says that God "has given us everything we need for a godly life" (2 Peter 1:3). He does the work for us, because we're incapable of doing it.

What is the key to making God happy? It is *not* trying to get our lives into perfect shape. The key to making God happy is to freely receive his salvation and then to willingly live in his love.

This was a life-changing revelation for me.

God loves me, not because I am so well-behaved, but because he chooses to love me! Jesus loves me and he wants us to work together!

He invites me to join with him, to be fully yoked with him. And it's not just a kind gesture on his part—Jesus is passionate about being yoked with me. In fact, he's so passionate that he came to earth, suffered, died the worst kind of death, and rose from the dead. Part of the salvation he offers to you and me is the promise of being with him in heaven.

What a relief! I could never measure up to God's standards, and Jesus knew that. Because he loved me, he did and continues to do all the hard work. Earning God's love is no longer my motivation for doing what God asks of me. Instead, my motivation comes from knowing God already loves me despite my sin.

Jesus said, "If you love me, you will keep my commands" (John 14:15). What a relief to realize that the key to keeping Jesus' commands is loving and following him day after day. I don't have to prove or earn anything.

I just have to walk alongside, yoked with the one who loves me.

HEAD SPACE

CONNECT WITH GOD

Here's a crazy exercise based on Romans 5:8, which tells us, "God demonstrates his own love for us, in that while we were still sinners, Christ died for us." Take a few minutes and try to think of every wrong thing you've ever done in your entire life. You might need another piece of paper (and a rock to climb under). Seriously though, start listing everything: lies, stealing, selfishness, lust, porn, gossip, getting trashed, cheating on an assignment—everything! After you're done, write, "God loves me!" next to each one. That's right. Jesus chose to love us while we were still sinners! At the end, take a few minutes to pray, asking for forgiveness and thanking Jesus for his love and friendship.

CONNECT WITH OTHERS

Jesus said, "Give as freely as you have received!" (Matthew 10:8 NLT). Along those lines, think of what God has freely given you—friends, family, opportunities, undeserved forgiveness, health—the list goes on. Now ask, *how does Jesus want me to freely give to others?* Below are a few examples:

- Freely give forgiveness
- Freely give friendship
- Freely give support
- Freely give money

Could there be someone in your life or community who could benefit from you giving "as you have received" from God? Who comes to mind? How, specifically, could you freely give to them?

HOW MIGHT I CHANGE?

> "Come to me, all of you who are weary and carry heavy burdens, and I will give you rest. Take my yoke upon you. Let me teach you, because I am humble and gentle at heart, and you will find rest for your souls." (Matthew 11:28–29 NLT)

I think what Jesus says here is so fascinating. Yokes are used on farms for more experienced animals to teach the young ones through being physically joined together. In this verse, Jesus is asking us to yoke, or join, with him as he loves and helps people. In essence, he's saying …

- Will you help someone feel loved?
- Will you be the physical expression of my comfort?
- Will you help someone to not feel lonely?

Take a minute and think about this amazing idea: God invites you to be the physical representation of his love to the people around you! Now, spend a few moments in prayer asking God to show you how you can join him in serving and expressing his love to others. Make a list of specific people, then for seven days commit to praying for them and their needs, asking God to use you to express his love to them in tangible ways.

CHAPTER 4

WRONG ASSUMPTION #4: GOD IS WAITING FOR ME TO MESS UP

≠

Remember the Christmas song "Santa Claus Is Coming to Town"? The one about being careful how you live because Santa is making a list of who's been naughty or nice?

That song captures an idea that many of us were raised with. You know—the concept that good things happen to good boys and girls, and bad things happen to bad boys and girls. If you're nice, and avoid doing anything on the "bad list" like hitting your sister or kicking the cat, and you somehow manage to pull that off all year long, then Santa Claus would bring you the new bicycle you've been asking for. On the other hand, if you're mean and kick the cat or hit your sister—or (being a dedicated Ohio boy) you cheer for the University of Michigan—Santa Claus would put a lump of coal in your stocking.

Somehow this influenced my assumptions about how God functions. In fact,

it seemed to me that the Bible even supported the idea that God operates by a system of retribution versus reward.

God is just waiting for us to mess up. For example, I found verses like these in the Bible: "The Lord has rewarded me according to my righteousness, according to the cleanness of my hands in his sight" (Psalm 18:24). And "You may be sure that your sin will find you out" (Numbers 32:23). To me, the message was crystal clear: if I sin, God will find out, and when he finds out, he'll get angry, and because he's angry, he'll mess up my life.

This concept is pretty common, and you may think this way, too. In fact, depending on your preconceived ideas about God, you may actually go as far as thinking that God *enjoys* punishing sinners. Many religious traditions teach this idea. Maybe you've heard someone say, "One day, those (fill in the blank) will get what's coming to them. They'll burn in hell. God is going to get even with them."

You would never think that way unless you assume God is out to get you. And you pretty much know you're in trouble already. Your God is making a list, checking it twice, finding out if you've been naughty or nice, and you're expecting to get your lump of coal. All because you've come to believe he's out to get you!

Payback Time

Anyone who walks around with that kind of preconceived idea about the heart and the mind of God is looking at life through a cracked lens.

Do the good things that happen to you in life come as a result of being such a good person? Conversely, do the bad things that happen to you in life result from being a bad person?

Is God simply a cosmic force who is monitoring it all? Is he observing and inspecting your behavior, waiting for you to mess up so he can bring punishment down on your head?

Many think it works something like this: everything good in life can be traced to having God's favor; everything bad results from failure to be good enough. The End.

Sound familiar? This belief system really messes up your relationship with God. Instead of wanting to know God's heart or God's mind, you'll start asking for God's rules. "Just give me the rules," you will say, "so I can follow every detail. That's how I'll stay away from punishment and difficulties."

Where all this really gets a little nuts is when you manage to follow the God-given rules and you develop an elevated view of yourself. *See, I'm not such a bad person*, you might think, *because I keep the rules.* When you view yourself as a good rule keeper—a good religious participant—you start to get a false assurance that you're good enough already, so you don't really need God after all. *I don't need to ask for his mercy, forgiveness, or compassion in my life because I've kept the rules. The evidence proves it: I've never cheered for Michigan! I've never gone to prison! I don't worship a statue of a false God.*

A Contractual Relationship with God

I end up believing that if I just honor God, keep the rules, and participate in my religion in the correct way, then God is obligated to be nice to me since I've been nice to him.

This sets up what I call a "contractual relationship" with God. Our contract reads something like this: If I do good things for God (I keep the rules), God is obligated to do good things for me (I won't lose my job, health, or hair). On the flip side, if I do bad things (I fail to keep the rules), bad things will happen to me (I'll lose my job, health, and hair).

This mindset about God takes people to some crazy places in their spiritual lives. One extreme is to throw your hands up and say, "I can never make God happy," which we talked about in the previous chapter. The other extreme is to become cultish in the way you respond to God, which we talked about under our first false assumption, "I Need to Work Harder to Make God Happy."

It's All about God

Here is a different approach: What if my point of view is off? What if *God* is supposed to be the focal point of my life, not me? What if God loves me and wants what's best for me? What if my relationship with God isn't supposed to be the way I've assumed it should be?

The correct view of God is this: I exist for God. God does not exist for me.

If God loves me (and he does), and if God's love is complete (and it is), then anything that happens in my life, positive or negative, happens under the complete control of a loving and powerful God.

When something positive occurs and I feel blessed, that thing did not take place because I earned it. And when something negative transpires and I'm concerned and anxious, it actually didn't happen to spite me. In fact, that negative thing turns out to be something I've been entrusted with.

There is a fascinating passage in the second part of the Bible, the New Testament, in the book of James:

Consider it pure joy, my brothers and sisters, whenever you face trials of many kinds, because you know that the testing of your faith produces perseverance. Let perseverance finish its work so that you may be mature and complete, not lacking anything. If any of you lacks wisdom, you should ask God, who gives generously to all without finding fault, and it will be given to you. But when you ask, you must believe and not doubt, because the one who doubts is like a wave of the sea, blown and tossed by the wind. That person should not expect to receive anything from the Lord. (James 1:2–7)

This passage provides an interesting glimpse into the mind of God. It explains that God looks at trials in my life as something he can trust me with, because they have a purpose. God is not waiting around for me to mess up. Actually, he's ready to give me strength and make me victorious in each trial I face. But his path to victory is almost always a different path than what I would choose. What God says in the book of James is that the path to victory runs right through the middle of trials.

When bad things happen in your life, it's not necessarily because God is punishing you. More likely, if you are seeking to be his disciple, God is using those difficulties to prepare you for greater things in your life. When you "consider it pure joy" as you face trials, you choose this mind-set because those trials will produce perseverance. Through hard circumstances, God will give you something you wouldn't be able to get on your own. He wants to give you what you need to become a stronger person and Christ follower.

The Way to Victory

Think of perseverance as spiritual endurance. You can count your trials as joy because through them you gain spiritual endurance, and after spiritual endurance finishes its work, you will be "mature and complete, not lacking anything." In other words,

God sees in you the potential to be a stronger person, and he gives you a trial in order to bring about complete maturity in you, enabling you to do what he's called you to do.

When I was a freshman in high school, I made the junior varsity baseball team. Our JV baseball coach was one of those hyper-intense coaches. He lived and breathed baseball. I think he even ate baseballs. He approached baseball as if we were going to war. He'd run us, work us, and push us so hard. I remember thinking, *Hey coach, relax. It's just JV baseball.*

One day after practice, the coach asked me to stay behind. I was working on becoming a pitcher because I was able to throw fairly hard for a high school freshman, but I'd never been able to throw a strike. In my mind, this was a small detail in the big game of baseball. After all, aren't strike zones basically suggestions, not hard and fast rules? But to my coach, not being able to throw a strike was one of the greater failings possible in modern-day society.

So, he held me back after practice and had me go to the pitching mound. I would throw a pitch, then he'd ask me to change my form. I'd throw a pitch, and he'd have me change the angle of release. I'd throw another pitch, then he'd have me work on footwork. This went on and on.

Finally, exhausted and exasperated after almost two hours of throwing pitch after pitch, only to be told I wasn't doing it right, I stopped and looked at the coach with fire in my eyes. "Why are you being such a jerk to me?" I asked. "I'm trying my best."

I'll never forget what my coach said back to me: "I'm not trying to be a jerk to you. I actually see great potential in your ability to be a pitcher. I'm trying to get that potential out of you!"

What a difference that made in how I viewed the trial. I'd been interpreting that after-practice session as punishment from my coach. *He must be out to get me. That's the way Coach is. Everybody knows he takes baseball too seriously.* But when I discovered the heart and mind of my coach, my perspective changed completely. He was not out to get me. Instead, he was seeking to mature me. He was not waiting for me to mess up. He was helping me refine my skills and ability. You might even say he was looking to help me become complete.

It's the same with God. He is not making a list and checking it twice so he can punish you with a lump of coal or reward you with a new bicycle. God is looking at your life and governing it through the directives of Scripture so you can be "mature and complete, not lacking anything."

And when God refines you, not only do you become the person he's called you to be, but you actually become the person you really want to be.

Heart and Mind

Now this can sound a bit confusing. That's why I love these verses in James chapter 1, especially verse 5: "If any of you lacks wisdom, you should ask God, who gives generously to all without finding fault, and it will be given to you."

I don't need to stay in the dark about what God is doing. When I don't understand the reason for a trial, I simply need to ask him. That's what I did with my baseball coach when I asked, "Why are you doing this to me?" Then he revealed his heart and mind to me.

When I ask God my questions, I can't ignore verses 6 and 7, as James makes clear: "But when you ask, you must believe and not doubt, because the one who doubts is like a wave of the sea, blown and tossed by the wind. That person should not expect to receive anything from the Lord."

What all this boils down to is more trust and faith. I put my trust and faith in the heart and mind of God. I must not doubt that God loves me and is accomplishing something greater than what I can see in my life right now. I must not doubt that he always has my best interests in mind … and that my *best* best interest is becoming more like Christ.

Is God waiting for you to mess up? No. He knows full well that's going to happen.

Is God looking to mature you and complete you to make you more and more like his Son, Jesus? Absolutely!

And when you trust his heart and mind, he'll continually strengthen your faith and make you more like him.

HEAD SPACE

CONNECT WITH GOD

The term *grace* that we find in the Bible is defined as: "God's unmerited favor." I like my friend Ezra's definition the best. He says, "Grace is God loving us just because he chooses to."

Reflect on what you've done or could do to deserve God's forgiveness. The truth is there's nothing you could do to earn the gift of Jesus because we don't measure up to the standards of God's perfect love. We all have to conclude that it's only by his grace and unconditional love that we have forgiveness available to us.

Make a list of all the things you've done this week that you might think would cause God to love you *less*. Next, make a list of the things you've done this week that you think might cause God to love you *more*. (I have to confess these are trick questions, because the answer to both is, *nothing*!)

In Ephesians 1:5–6, Paul wrote that God "predestined us to adoption as sons through Jesus Christ to Himself ... to the praise of the glory of His grace, which He freely bestowed on us in [Jesus]" (NASB). Did you catch that? He *freely* bestows his grace on us! There's nothing that will cause God to love us more or less, because he loves us based on *his* goodness, not based on what *we* do or don't do. *This* is unconditional love—that God shows us undeserved grace, simply because he chooses to.

Take a couple of minutes to thank God for this undeserved grace.

CONNECT WITH OTHERS

For this next exercise, I really encourage you to take an extended amount of time to meditate on Psalm 50:23: "He who offers a sacrifice of thanksgiving honors Me" (NASB). Then take this challenge: Keep a list throughout an entire day of all you have to be thankful for. The Bible says all good and perfect things come from above (James 1:17). In other words, everything good in your life is a gift from God! When you remember that we only deserve judgment for our sin and separation from God in hell, the list of good things (air, water, joy, Ohio State football) gets pretty long.

This "attitude of gratitude" will help you become closer to God because you'll recognize the abundance of his love in every part of your life. This same attitude changes our relationships with the people around us:

- I can serve people with joy ... because I am loved by God.
- I can quickly forgive people ... because I am forgiven by God.
- I can be generous to people ... because God is so generous to me.

You get the idea. My view of God directly affects my view of people.

HOW MIGHT I CHANGE?

A couple of questions to ask yourself: *What would I be like if I actually let God define and control my entire life? What could it look like to live with the recognition that, God is God, and I am not God?*

By reading the Bible we can learn more about Jesus. We learn things like:

+ His *mind-set* is higher than ours. (Isaiah 55:8)
+ His *actions* are characterized by perfection, and he never has bad motives. (Galatians 5:19–24)
+ His *attitude* is characterized by humility and thinking more highly of others than he thinks of himself. (Philippians 2:3–7)
+ His *priorities* focus on loving his Father, loving people, and conveying the gospel so others can embrace him and these priorities. (Matthew 22:37–40; 28:19–20)

Letting "God be God" will impact my mind-set, actions, attitudes, and priorities.

Following him is characterized by living out the words of John the Baptist: "[Jesus] must become greater; I must become less" (John 3:30). When God becomes your first priority, you start to reflect the attitude and mind-set of Jesus. What could it look like to live each day, displaying God's mind-set, actions, attitudes, and priorities?

Stop and think through how John 3:30 can show up in your life:

- Jesus' attitude of humility and pattern of thinking of others first could look like …
- Jesus' priority of love toward God and others could be expressed if I …

CHAPTER 5

WRONG ASSUMPTION #5: JESUS IS FOR KIDS

≠

Have you ever walked into a Christian knickknack shop, bookstore, or discount store, only to run across what I affectionately call, "Jesus junk"? You know, those cute little figurines—Jesus playing soccer with a little boy or coaching a couple of little ballerinas. I've even seen soft Jesus dolls that children can take to bed at night, so they can snuggle with Jesus as they go to sleep. My friend Joe bought me a grilled cheese maker called a "Grilled Cheesus." It had an electronic sandwich press that burned a portrait of Jesus into the toast … true story!

Many times Jesus is presented as someone who helps children not have bad dreams, or the person children sing "Happy Birthday" to at Christmastime. People often talk about children's need for Jesus. Parents discuss the importance of Sunday school and read picture books to their kids to teach them Bible stories about Noah's Ark, David and Goliath, and baby Jesus in the manger. We want to help kids understand God and that's the normal way to do it.

However, at a certain point, it's normal to grow out of a storybook approach to understanding God. Many kids who've been exposed to lots of religious conversation and activity in their homes stop having much to do with organized religion when they get into high school or college. The statistics are staggering. It happens all the time.

Young people may go to church their entire lives and be heavily involved in youth groups, only to move into their young adult years and forget all about God.

The One-Dimensional Jesus

Sadly, many children are taught to have simplistic faith that amounts to some version of "God said it, I believe it, and that's good enough for me." Rarely are kids taught how to engage real issues or think critically about portions of the Bible that are hard to understand. No wonder the faith of young adults is so easily discounted and debunked once they leave home. Their experience and interaction with Jesus may only have consisted of shallow social activities undertaken because of family pressure. Their faith has never been put to a real, critical test. So when young adults find themselves in a situation where they actually have to act on what they've claimed to believe, their belief system is called into question and their faith collapses.

This pattern is tied, in part anyway, to the portrayal of Jesus as someone who is just for kids. Too often we talk about Jesus in ways that are meant to appeal to children. Or we talk about Jesus in only feminine terms, instead of holistically (the very best of femininity and masculinity). Just think about how we portray "love" in our culture. It's the love of Mama, or boyfriends and girlfriends, or of close friends and baby animals. The message of love is even portrayed as someone in a tie-dye t-shirt with flowers in her hair, dancing in a field of daisies.

Is that what John meant when he wrote, "God is love" (1 John 4:8)?

Even when we make the connection between God and love, we rarely use adult terms.

We think about Jesus as being more like a nanny than a gladiator.

We think of him as a soft-spoken, kind-hearted, fairly spineless man and not as an aggressive, self-sacrificial, rock-solid rescuer of the innocent and the oppressed.

With so many childish and cartoonish images being presented about God, a very fair conclusion would be that God is merely a childish notion that should be outgrown. Adults no longer need anyone to tuck them in at night. They no longer need to fold their hands, squint their eyes, and say thank you for their ice cream. Since they're not afraid of the dark and can think for themselves (and since other people tend to devalue a relationship with God anyway), then of course it's logical for grown adults to view God in the past tense and to get busy solving their own problems, isn't it? Why would anybody rely on a soccer-buddy God? What adult would want to follow a Jesus that cartoon vegetables sing about? It's good to allow our thinking to mature, but sometimes we end up throwing the baby out with the bathwater.

Christ the Warrior King

What if we began to think of Jesus differently? What if we let our view of him be formed from the Bible and not from the "Jesus junk"? I'll bet that studying the Bible would go a long way toward rounding out your picture of God. That's the best way to get a clear view of the heart and mind of God, especially when you look at the life and death of his Son, Jesus.

The Jesus in the Bible looks very *little* like your typical children's book character.

The more you read about him, the better you'll understand that Jesus is by far the strongest man you've ever seen. He is courageous, passionate, and determined. Even his silence is powerful.

Just think about Jesus' crucifixion. You can read firsthand accounts about it in the Bible. One account can be found in chapters 22 through 24 of the book of Luke. (There are parallel accounts of the crucifixion also found in Matthew 26–28, Mark 14–16, and John 18–21.) I guarantee that when you read this account, you'll never think of a jolly fellow out playing soccer with a bunch of little kids. Instead, you'll think of a medal-of-honor winner, a true hero who voluntarily gave his life to rescue the innocent.

When Jesus was betrayed by his friend Judas into the hands of the Roman soldiers, he was "led like a lamb to the slaughter, and as a sheep before its shearers is silent, so he did not open his mouth" (Isaiah 53:7). Was he like a clueless sheep—fearful, uncertain, and easily cowed? Did He accidentally find himself caught up in a political firestorm at a difficult historical moment, only to die in the mix? No, Jesus is called the Lamb of God, in part because he allowed himself to be captured without fighting back, just as a lamb might do. He knew what he was doing, and he could have escaped if he had wanted.

But he didn't.

Jesus says this: "The reason my Father loves me is that I lay down my life—only to take it up again. No one takes it from me, but I lay it down of my own accord. I have authority to lay it down and authority to take it up again. This command I received from my Father" (John 10:17–18).

Jesus was not a foolish man caught in a political conflict. Jesus is the Lamb of God offering himself as the ultimate sacrifice for the sake of people he loved.

> **Jesus is the firefighter who runs into the burning building; the marine who falls on the grenade to save his buddies; the one who, by his own authority, laid down his life to rescue every human being from the spiritual death that they ultimately deserved as a result of their sin.**

As the crucifixion narrative plays out, you see the absolute strength of Jesus again and again. When Pilate asks, "Are you the king of the Jews?" Jesus simply indicates, "You have said so" (Matthew 27:11). When given the opportunity to argue or defend himself to the elders and chief priests, he says nothing.

We see it go down like this: "Then Pilate asked him, 'Don't you hear the testimony they are bringing against you?' But Jesus made no reply, not even to a single charge—to the great amazement of the governor" (13–14).

> **Jesus' goal was not to get out of the pain. His goal was to win the battle for the hearts and souls of humanity.**

No Greater Love

When you watch what happens next, the strength, power, and courage of Jesus become undeniable. This is what you see:

First, he was mocked, spat upon, and beaten—and this was no light beating. When the Romans beat someone they inflicted the maximum amount of pain and suffering. Jesus was tied to a post and whipped. At the ends of their leather whipping straps, the Romans would attach pieces of bone, jagged glass, or metal. That meant, when they threw the whip, it would wrap around the victim's back and embed itself in his flesh, pulling off chunks of flesh as it was removed. Over and over, mercilessly, Jesus was whipped. By the time Jesus' bloody beating was finished, most assuredly his flesh would have been flayed all the way to the bone in places. He would have suffered extreme blood loss, and his body would have started going into shock.

After that savage beating, he was taken off the whipping post and cruelly ridiculed by the Roman soldiers. They ripped at his face and pulled at his beard. One of them fashioned a thorny crown and pressed it into the skin of his head. These thorns would have been long and very sharp, perhaps even an inch in length, and when the crown was forced down on Jesus' head they would have punctured his flesh deeply, scraping all the way down to the skull and ripping through sensitive nerve endings. Have you ever cut or hit your head? The pain can be excruciating. Magnify that pain and compound it with helpless humiliation. We learn more from Matthew's account:

> Then the governor's soldiers took Jesus into the Praetorium and gathered the whole company of soldiers around him. They stripped him and put a scarlet robe on him, and then twisted together a crown of thorns and set it on his head. They put a staff in his right hand. Then they knelt in front of him and mocked him. "Hail, king of the Jews!" they said. They spit on him, and took the staff and struck him on the head again and again. After they had mocked him, they took off the robe and put his own clothes on him. Then they led him away to crucify him. (Matthew 27:27–31)

The robe would have soaked up and clotted the blood from his back and shoulders, caking it with dirt. When it was removed, his fresh scabs would have been torn and the wounds reopened. Jesus had not slept since being arrested the night before and now, in the hot midday sun, his body was reaching the limits of human frailty.

Even with all he had endured, this man somehow found within himself the strength to struggle to his feet, pick up the heavy wooden crosspiece that was forced on him, and begin the journey to his place of execution. As he staggered through the streets, he would have been spat upon, poked, and jeered at by the same crowds who, only a few days before, had triumphantly cheered his entry into Jerusalem. It was humiliation heaped upon humiliation, pain heaped upon pain, with even more to follow.

Don't forget, he could've escaped at any moment. Jesus had countless angels at his beck and call.

But, obedient to his Father's wishes, Jesus endured everything in order to see it through. Jesus loved you and me so deeply that he chose to go through with the terrible pain and humiliation that would lead to his death, but would also lead to the complete forgiveness of all our sins.

At the place of crucifixion, the cross was laid in the dirt. Jesus was thrown onto his bleeding back against the rough wood while spikes were driven through his hands and feet with brutal force. When the cross was raised into its upright position, the full weight of his body would have pressed onto the spikes, causing him to instinctively try to relieve the crushing pain by pushing up against the spike that had been driven through both feet, dragging the torn and bleeding flesh of his back across the rough wood of the cross. Every moment was excruciating. At this point, the relief of death could hardly come soon enough.

Even while bleeding profusely and enduring hours of unimaginable pain, Jesus still cared enough to talk with one of the two thieves being crucified next to him, assuring him of his heavenly destination:

> One of the criminals who hung there hurled insults at him: "Aren't you the Messiah? Save yourself and us!"
>
> But the other criminal rebuked him. "Don't you fear God," he said, "since you are under the same sentence? We are punished justly, for we are getting what our deeds deserve. But this man has done nothing wrong."
>
> Then he said, "Jesus, remember me when you come into your kingdom."
>
> Jesus answered him, "Truly I tell you, today you will be with me in paradise." (Luke 23:39–43)

Eventually, the man's lungs filled with fluid and he suffocated.

> At three in the afternoon Jesus cried out in a loud voice, "Eloi, Eloi, lema sabachthani?" (which means "My God, my God, why have you forsaken me?") … With a loud cry, Jesus breathed his last. (Mark 15:34, 37)

That's the *real* Jesus. Does that sound like a snuggly guy whose job is to keep little kids from having bad dreams at night? Does that sound like someone who'd dance through a field with flowers in his hair, singing about love and peace?

Or does that sound like the bravest, strongest man you've

ever heard of—someone whose grit and determination defy description?

Heroic Love

To be honest, I don't have much interest in following a God in order to learn to be nice to people. I can probably figure that one out on my own or by watching a few episodes of *Sesame Street*. But I am more than interested in a God who sacrificed himself in order to rescue me. I am interested in a God who's so relentless in his love, and unflinching in his dedication, that he would give his life for me. And then, to show that he truly is God, he would come back to life again. Yes, I'm interested. This is not the same person as Mr. Jesus Nice Guy, who's just for kids.

When this difference first started to register with me, it gave me the courage and determination not to be embarrassed about being a follower of Jesus. I started to take pride in who Jesus is and what he did for me. And I began to understand that this God would never leave me or forsake me, but would always help me do whatever he asked me to do.

My wife, Heidi, told me a story from when she was a little girl. She was in a river in her home country, Brazil. She and her friends were swimming upstream from a large waterfall. They were far enough away that there was no danger of being swept away by the currents—or so everyone thought. Heidi was in an inner tube, floating lazily down the river, daydreaming and enjoying the sunshine and scenery. Having lost track of time and space, she suddenly realized she had long passed the point where she should've gotten out of the river. The strong currents began to pull the inner tube toward the waterfall.

As she was trying to orient herself to the danger she might be in, the inner tube bumped a log stuck in the river and Heidi slipped through the middle of the tube. Now the danger she was in started to register in her mind. Heidi slipped under the water, then pulled herself back up, only to slip through the middle of the tube again. Heart racing and mind turning, she realized she was in grave danger and started to fight for her life.

Unbeknownst to her, her father had seen this desperate situation playing out and when he realized the danger his little girl was in, he began to run to her. The path between the two of them was filled with rough water and a jagged rock protruding out of the river. Her father, fighting the current, pushed past the rock and pressed toward his little girl. Without thought of his own life and safety, he fought to rescue his daughter.

Heidi remembers seeing her father running and calling out to her every time she struggled to the surface. She says what struck her most was that her father had become bloodied by the rocks. In his determination to rescue his child, he was undeterred by the fact that the rocks had cut him, bruised him, and torn his flesh. His pursuit was unbroken!

This is God: a fearless Father who recognizes the desperation of his children long before they do, braving pain, suffering, and extreme peril in order to grab hold of the ones he loves.

Is Jesus for kids? Yes, of course he is. He's for everybody, both young and old. But he looks like Heidi's dad, not the pictures you see of Jesus in a white robe, sitting in a field of daisies, hopelessly separated from reality. Would he play soccer with his children? Sure. Would he battle through earth, time, space, and hell itself to save them? Absolutely.

HEAD SPACE

CONNECT WITH GOD

In John 10:17 Jesus said, "I lay down my life—only to take it up again!" He chose to give his life so he could gain yours. Jesus' death was payment for our sin, so when he defeated death, he was also defeating our sin. What's more, 2 Corinthians 5:21 tells us, "God made him who had no sin to be sin for us, so that in him we might become the righteousness of God." Since it was *our* sin that Jesus died for, his victory over sin is *our* victory too! Jesus agreed to become our Savior, uniting us with himself. If you've decided to follow Jesus, it's as if you're on Jesus' team—everything Jesus does is attributed to you because of your relationship with him.

Pause and consider Jesus' words to his Father as he was hanging on a cross by spikes in his hands and feet: "My God, my God, why have you forsaken me?" (Matthew 27:46). As Jesus took our sin on himself, he was separated from his perfect Father. Then Christ, through the Holy Spirit, would take up his life again! Think about that! Why did Jesus become sin—or, more personally, for whom did he do it? Who benefits from his resurrection?

It's powerful to remember that if Jesus didn't need to die for any other person in the whole world, he still would've died for you—and he *did* die for you! Now chew on this idea: Not only did he die for you, but he was raised for you! He laid down his life—and took it up again—for you! What emotions are triggered in your heart and mind when you really think that through on a deep level? Share these feelings with God. Then, give thanks for

his initiative in coming to rescue you: *Lord, I am so grateful that*
_____.

CONNECT WITH OTHERS

> And this same God who takes care of me will supply all
> your needs from his glorious riches. (Philippians 4:19 NLT)

God is a need-meeting God. He will provide for all of your needs—sometimes directly through the Holy Spirit, and at other times, through other people he sends your way. Our role is to gratefully receive from God without demanding or dictating *how* he will provide.

Get this picture in your mind:

You're grabbing coffee with Jesus again. As you get into the conversation, you start telling him about your needs and the things that matter most to you. You talk about parts of your life where you struggle, your strained relationships, or unfulfilled hopes. Now think how he might respond. He might listen to what's going on, affirm the struggle, offer wisdom, or pray with you. In the fashion of a true friend, Jesus wouldn't always tell you what you *want* to hear, but he'd tell you what you *need* to hear. He'd be honest with you, all the while loving you where you're at. He might plan to meet up later to check in, or even to help with the next step in what you're going through. However the scene plays out, Jesus would address your needs.

Take some time to talk with God: *God, I need You to provide*
_____. *You've promised to provide all my needs,*
so I am trusting You to _____.

Jesus' hope is that you would love others as you have been loved by him. Ask God to bring specific people or needs to your mind so you can be used by God to meet those needs. Then make a list as you pray.

HOW MIGHT I CHANGE?

Look at these verses:

- This is real love—not that we loved God, but that he loved us and sent his Son as a sacrifice to take away our sin. (1 John 4:10 NLT)
- There is no greater love than to lay down one's life for one's friends. (John 15:13 NLT)

Jesus' sacrifice on the cross shows that God views us with immense worth. Imagine God is speaking specifically to you in this verse, saying, *I rescued you because I love you and couldn't bear the thought of not having a relationship with you. That's how I see you: one who is worth my sacrifice.*

So many things are competing for their place as our identity—net worth, grades, youth, athletics, childhood baggage, social status … The list is endless! Take a minute to download the idea that our Creator, our Savior, the God of the universe, loves you and finds you valuable enough to make the ultimate sacrifice of his Son. Wow! Finally, consider this: How does this declaration of worth change how you see yourself, how you invest your life, and how you see the people around you?

FINAL THOUGHTS

AHA MOMENTS

≠

$\neq$

Have you ever had an aha moment? I've had a few in my life. The day I met Heidi was certainly one of them. I could've married that girl the day I met her! I waited for a while, of course. But I certainly had one of those aha moments that day. When I was in college, I remember asking people, "How will I know I've met *the one*?" And the answer I got from married people who were in love was, "You'll just know." I always thought that was the dumbest answer until I met Heidi. And when I met her, I *just knew*. Aha! She's the one!

Challenging My Assumptions

Another one of my greatest aha moments happened when I was talking to my friend David Ferguson. One day we were discussing what the heart and mind of God is like. David was introducing me to some new ideas about how to "hear" God and challenging me on some of my assumptions about him. But before I share what he told me, first let me give you a little background.

A verse of Scripture I quoted a lot was John 14:15, in which Jesus says, "If you love Me, you will keep My commandments"

(NASB). I grew up hearing that verse replay itself in my mind again and again and again: *If you love me, you will keep my commandments.* I was taught that what Jesus meant was, if you loved him, you would do what he said to do: "Keep my commandments."

So that's what I did. I spent my energy working to obey what I was thought were his commandments. I wanted to know the rules, I wanted to keep the rules, and I thought I could make God happy that way. Even after I became a pastor and a teacher, I taught people that "obedience is God's love language," and what God wants from us, more than anything, is for us to obey him.

As I expressed this to my friend David, he asked me a very simple question that radically changed my life: "What if Jesus *didn't* say it that way?"

Startled, I looked at him and said, "What do you mean? That's exactly what the verse says: 'If you love me, you will *keep* my commandments.'"

"What if you're hearing it wrong?" David responded. "What if Jesus said, 'If you *love* me, you will keep my commandments'?"

Jesus was saying that if we learn to love him, the rules will take care of themselves. He was teaching that love and obedience go hand in hand, and when we learn to love, we'll be eager to obey—all on our own.

What a huge aha moment of my life!

Jesus was not urging me to obey, obey, obey, after all. He was saying that my "work" is *loving* him.

Not a kid's love, not hippie love, but a Navy Seal-type love. A love so intense that I would give my life for my brother. A love so powerful that I would seek to rescue those who are suffering injustice. A love that wants to know the heart and mind of God so deeply that I follow him closely.

God's emphasis was on *love* more than obedience. It was as if I could suddenly hear Jesus saying, *Jeff, if you love me ... you will wind up doing the things I have asked you to do.*

The Heart of the Matter

What about you? If God desires your love most of all, that means he cares about your heart the most.

God cares more about your heart than he cares about your compliance, religion, or good behavior. He knows if he has your heart, the rest will follow.

What if God *enjoys* you and wants to be with you? He knows that as your love for him grows, you'll find yourself doing what he wants you to do, simply because of your love for him. You'll start loving the people he loves. You'll love them enough to alter your behavior toward them and even *give* to them.

The fact is, when you love Jesus you'll love people too. In the Bible, we read about the time when someone asked Jesus to explain what it means to follow him. Jesus didn't have to think very hard. Essentially he answered, "Okay, here's what following me boils down to." The most important command, Jesus said is this:

> Love the Lord your God with all your heart and with all your soul and with all your mind and with all your strength.' The second is this: 'Love your neighbor as yourself.' There is no commandment greater than these." (Mark 12:29–31)

Those words came straight out of Jesus' heart and mind. God wants one thing from you and me: our love. He wants us to love him with everything we have. And that love is always going to be expressed through our love for other people, because people are the ones Jesus loves. When I love God I will love people, and when I love people, my love for God will deepen. In loving God, I'll see the needs of others and seek to meet those needs. As I recognize their needs and understand the commitment it takes to meet them, I'll recognize I have those same needs and see how God meets my needs on a deeper and deeper level.

Focus on Love

The key to a relationship with God is love, not obedience. It was an aha moment when I realized I had my basic assumption backward, and it affected all of my other assumptions. I had assumed God was a hard-to-please taskmaster who would never be happy with me. No wonder I felt stressed out about the whole Christian life.

Now things are a lot simpler for me: I love God.

In response, his life and love keep growing in my heart, and I find myself wanting to obey everything he's outlined for me to follow. Now I'm able to love other people with the overflow of his love—and love God deeper in the process.

What about you? Does your perspective match up with reality? How has your perspective affected the way you interact with God and others? If you considered a different perspective, what could happen?

This is a great moment to stop and think, with clear to-dos … like read the book of John, or interact with JeffBogue.org for more conversations, media, and thoughts around these topics.

Could God, perhaps, open *your* heart and mind to a whole new way of understanding *his* heart and mind?

CONNECT WITH GOD

Here are only three of many false views people have of God:

- ◆ He is constantly inspecting us
- ◆ He is disappointed with us
- ◆ He is distant

Can you relate?

False view #1: God Is Constantly Inspecting Us

As you read the Bible or think about God, you might imagine a tone of expectation and demand. The words might carry a questioning tone, conveying the sense that there's a test to be passed in every area of life. Or perhaps you haven't read the Bible much yourself, but you've seen people on the street or television who claim to live from the Bible, so you've imagined God shaking his finger at you as he speaks. His stern tone and gestures are a reminder of his constant inspection.

False View #2: God Is Disappointed with Us

As you read the Bible, do you hear a voice that seems full of dissatisfaction? This kind of God might look down at you with arms crossed, shaking his head, saying, *If you really loved me, then you would be able to keep my commandments. In fact, I have known all along that you didn't really love me, and what you just did proves it!* Maybe you find yourself examining everything you do, think, or say as if you might slip up at any moment, causing God to be disappointed with you.

False View #3: God Is Distant

When you read the Bible, the voice you hear may seem cold or disinterested. This kind of God might seem preoccupied with other things or more important people. You picture him looking up, absent-mindedly saying:

If you love me, then you'll probably keep my commandments. Thanks for stopping by. Let me look you up and see what you have done with your life … What's the name?

But what if you understood God differently?

Could it be that when you woke up this morning, God was longing for you to love him? And do you think, perhaps, God knew all along that if someone loves him, they naturally end up following his commandments as they experience perfect love?

The real Jesus is not inspecting, disappointed, or distant. He's excited to be with you, be recognized by you, love you, and receive love from you! He's excited to be your friend. He wants what's best for you and doesn't want you to miss the joy that comes from a relationship with him.

Stop and think through times you *didn't* see God as being excited to love you. I encourage you to talk this through with a friend or group of friends, and even pray for each other that you'd be able to start seeing Jesus as he really is—a Jesus that's excited to love you!

CONNECT WITH OTHERS

When you consider the different ways we "hear" God, it's important to realize that our understanding of God directly affects our interactions with other people. We often interact with others the way we believe God is interacting with us. For instance, if you think God is always inspecting your life, waiting for you to mess up, you might be tempted to look at other people through an inspecting lens as well. If you perceive God to be distant and cold, you might be tempted to be distant from others and not be open with your faith or life. The bottom line is this: how you understand God directly affects your relationships with the people around you.

Think for a few minutes about how your understanding of God might positively or negatively affect your relationships.

HOW MIGHT I CHANGE?

Consider what Scripture says about God's love for us:

- ◆ God demonstrated his love for us by sending Jesus to die for us while we were still sinners. (Romans 5:8)
- ◆ Nothing can separate us from God's love. (Romans 8:38–39)
- ◆ He's poured out his love on us through the Holy Spirit. (Romans 5:5)
- ◆ The love of Jesus for us is infinitely great and surpasses knowledge. (Ephesians 3:18–19)
- ◆ Because of his great love for us, God made us alive with Jesus. (Ephesians 2:4–5)

Jesus left the disciples with exact instructions explaining how the world was to know about him. Jesus' intent was that people would believe in God's love because of the example of Christ followers who truly loved one another.

Think through some ways that you can "speak" love to people today:

- Say something encouraging.
- Say something comforting.
- Say something affirming.

Whether you say it, text it, or mail a hand-written note ... Share Jesus' love with someone today!

Acknowledgments

When you work on a big project there are always so many people who influence your thoughts and life that deserve more thanks than you could ever give them, but I will try.

Heidi and my family, your support, love, and help mean the world to me. I love you all more deeply than words could ever express. I am so proud of you all!

David Ferguson, thank you for your belief in me and support of this project. You've taught me so much about the head and heart of Christ. Thank you for your friendship, mentorship, and partnership in all our ministry efforts.

Dave Bellis, you've influenced my life more than you will ever know and I love you for it.

Laura Aman, your countless hours of work and passion for the message of this book are above and beyond any job description. This project literally would never have happened without you! Thank you for your passion for your generation. Your work and heart are affecting the lives of thousands of people. They will most likely give me too much credit for *your* work, but I want everyone to know your commitment is the reason for the success of this project!

Terri Baird, your servant's heart and dedication to God's work is unmatched. Thank you for being such a great teammate!

Carlton Garborg, David Sluka, and the team at Broad-Street Publishing, thank you for investing in the dream. I am grateful for your support and partnership.

Grace Church staff, I am proud of you all and deeply grateful that we get to serve the kingdom together and chase the dreams God has placed in our hearts.

Grace Church family, you took in a twenty-two-year-old kid and allowed me to try, fail, and try again. I am so grateful God is allowing Heidi and me to invest our lives with you for the work of the kingdom! I am grateful and honored to serve together with you!

About the Author

D r. Jeff Bogue is a pastor whose passion is to help Jesus make sense to everyone. Jeff became a Christ follower when he was a junior in college and has been married to his soul mate, Heidi, for twenty-three years. His passion comes from his own experience of searching for the mind and heart of God, and being completely changed by what he discovered.

Jeff is a graduate of Grace College and Seminary in Winona Lake, Indiana. He's had the privilege of sharing life with the people of Grace Church of Greater Akron, Ohio, for the past twenty-three years. Jeff loves his family and friends and is grateful he's been able to take his life journey with such amazing people. Leading the church to love and serve the people around them energizes him.

Jeff and Heidi have six wonderful kids: five crazy boys and one "Sweet Baby" princess. Alongside their kids, they work to express God's love all over the world. One of Jeff's greatest joys is serving together with his family. Wherever the Bogues go, they see not only a desperate need for the compassion and mercy of Christ to be expressed through meeting people's physical needs, but also the hope of Christ's message of salvation for the soul.

Connect with Jeff at JeffBogue.org.

About Grace Church

Grace Church began in the mid-1940s as a Bible study in Barberton, Ohio. In 1958, the group joined in the National Fellowship of Grace Brethren Churches. It's now a thriving multi-site church of more than eight thousand people, with new campuses starting in the United States and beyond.

Senior Pastor, Dr. Jeff Bogue, says, "The church is full of ordinary people trying to live extraordinary lives. At some point, someone shared the story of Jesus with each of us, and we believe that knowing him is the key to a meaningful, purpose-filled life."

Grace's mission is to know the gospel (the story of Jesus), share it, and live it out. As church leaders and other members put it, we strive to "Know it. Live it. Give it away." The story of Jesus is the heartbeat of Grace Church.

For more info or to check out additional resources, visit Graceohio.org.

The Great Commandment Network

The Great Commandment Network is an international collaborative network of strategic Kingdom leaders from the faith community, marketplace, education, and caregiving fields who prioritize the powerful simplicity of the words of Jesus to love God, love others, and see others become His followers (Matthew 22:37–40; 28:19–20).

The Great Commandment Network is served through the following:

- The Center for Relational Leadership: Their mission is to teach, train, and mentor both ministry and corporate leaders in Great Commandment principles, seeking to equip leaders with relational skills so they might lead as Jesus led.
- The Galatians 6:6 Retreat Ministry: This ministry offers a unique two-day retreat for ministers and their spouses for personal renewal while reestablishing and affirming ministry and family priorities.
- The Center for Relational Care (CRC): The CRC provides therapy and support to relationships in crisis through an accelerated process of growth and healing, including "Relational Care Intensives" for couples, families, and singles.

For more information on how you, your church, ministry, denomination, or movement can be served by the Great Commandment Network, write or call:

Great Commandment Network
2511 South Lakeline Blvd.
Cedar Park, TX 78613
1-800-881-8008
GreatCommandment.net

JeffBogue.org